ASHLEY TISDALE

Mitchell Lane
PUBLISHERS

P.O. Box 196
Hockessin, Delaware 19707
Visit us on the web: www.mitchelllane.com
Comments? email us: mitchelllane@mitchelllane.com

Mitchell Lane PUBLISHERS

Copyright © 2009 by Mitchell Lane Publishers. All rights reserved. No part of this book may be reproduced without written permission from the publisher. Printed and bound in the United States of America.

Printing   1   2   3   4   5   6   7   8   9

A Robbie Reader
Contemporary Biography

Albert Pujols	Alex Rodriguez	Aly and AJ
Amanda Bynes	**Ashley Tisdale**	Brittany Murphy
Charles Schulz	Dakota Fanning	Dale Earnhardt Jr.
Donovan McNabb	Drake Bell & Josh Peck	Dr. Seuss
Dwayne "The Rock" Johnson	Dylan & Cole Sprouse	Eli Manning
Hilary Duff	Jamie Lynn Spears	Jessie McCartney
Johnny Gruelle	The Jonas Brothers	Jordin Sparks
LeBron James	Mia Hamm	Miley Cyrus
Miranda Cosgrove	Raven-Symone	Shaquille O'Neal
The Story of Harley-Davidson	Syd Hoff	Tiki Barber
Tom Brady	Tony Hawk	

Library of Congress Cataloging-in-Publication Data
Mattern, Joanne, 1963–
 Ashley Tisdale / by Joanne Mattern.
    p. cm. — (A Robbie reader)
 Includes bibliographical references, discography, filmography and index.
 ISBN 978-1-58415-719-9 (library bound)
 1. Tisdale, Ashley—Juvenile literature. 2. Actors—United States—Biography—
Juvenile literature. I. Title.
 PN2287.T57M38 2009
 791.4302'8092—dc22
 [B]
                                                                    2008008066

ABOUT THE AUTHOR: Joanne Mattern is the author of more than 250 books for children. She has written biographies about many famous people for Mitchell Lane, including *Peyton Manning, The Jonas Brothers, LeBron James,* and *Drake Bell and Josh Peck.* Joanne also enjoys writing about animals, reading, and being outdoors. She lives in New York State with her husband, four children, and several pets.

PUBLISHER'S NOTE: The following story has been thoroughly researched and to the best of our knowledge represents a true story. While every possible effort has been made to ensure accuracy, the publisher will not assume liability for damages caused by inaccuracies in the data, and makes no warranty on the accuracy of the information contained herein. This story has not been authorized or endorsed by Ashley Tisdale.

PLB

TABLE OF CONTENTS

Words in **bold** type can be found in the glossary.

Ashley Tisdale became famous as an actress, but she is also a talented and confident singer with a hit CD. She delighted fans when she performed on MTV's *Total Request Live* in October 2007.

A New Look

Ashley Tisdale could not breathe. The actress from the Disney Channel's *High School Musical* and *The Suite Life of Zack and Cody* had always had a problem with her nose. It was crooked and blocked on one side. Her nose had also been broken two times. "My nose was to the left of my face," Ashley said. "There was something not right."

One night, while Ashley was performing on the *High School Musical* **tour**, she got sick backstage. A doctor had to help her breathe. Ashley knew she had to get help. She asked a doctor to fix her nose.

In 2007, many people criticized Ashley for getting a nose job. When she appeared at New York radio station Z100's Jingle Ball concert in December 2007, Ashley was surprised and hurt when people said her nose looked funny.

Actresses and other performers know that people are always looking at them and talking about them. There is a lot of pressure to look a certain way, and many of them have **surgery** to change their appearance. Would Ashley's fans think less of her if she changed her nose?

Ashley did not worry about what other people thought. She had her surgery on November 30, 2007. Just two weeks later, she appeared at a concert in New York City. Her nose was still healing and was swollen. Her fans got very upset. Newspapers and web sites made fun of her. They said her nose job was a mistake.

Ashley felt the comments were unfair. "I was still recovering!" she complained. "That's not what I look like."

Even though people made fun of her new nose, Ashley looked and felt better than ever. She was also glad she had been honest about having her nose fixed. Many **celebrities** who have surgery will not tell the truth. "I didn't want to play a game of **denying** it," Ashley said. "I wanted my fans to know."

Ashley's honesty and concern for her fans have always been part of her personality. These qualities helped her become one of today's most popular young stars.

When Ashley first went to Hollywood, a talent agency said she was really sweet but would never make it in Hollywood. Tisdale proved them wrong when she became famous on the Disney Channel show *The Suite Life of Zack and Cody.*

**CHAPTER
TWO**

One Day at the Mall

Ashley Michelle Tisdale was born on July 2, 1985. She grew up in the small town of West Deal, New Jersey. Ashley's parents are Mike and Lisa Tisdale. She has an older sister named Jennifer.

Ashley's family was very ordinary. However, they did have some famous relatives. Ashley's grandfather, Arnold Morris, developed Ginsu knives. These are especially sharp knives used for cooking. They were advertised in funny commercials that showed chefs using the knives to cut tin cans and pieces of rubber.

CHAPTER TWO

Ashley is also related to Ron Popeil, who also invented unusual products that were advertised on television. Some of his products were a vegetable chopper called the Veg-O-Matic and the Inside-the-Shell Egg Scrambler.

Ashley and her sister had a happy, quiet childhood. Ashley especially enjoyed music. "I have a really good ear with music," she

Ashley (left) is very close to her big sister, Jennifer. Jennifer is also an actress, and Ashley hopes to work with her someday.

explained. "I can play piano by ear, which means I can listen to a song and play it on the piano."

One day, Lisa Tisdale took Ashley to the Monmouth Mall in New Jersey. A huge crowd was gathered there to see Bill Perlman, who owned New Talent Management. He was looking for children who could be models or performers.

Ashley's mom did not stop in to see Perlman—but Perlman saw the Tisdales. He followed them into a store and asked them to take part in his talent search. Lisa said, "No, thank you," and continued shopping.

Perlman did not give up that easily. Later, he saw the Tisdales shopping in another part of the mall. He gave Lisa a business card and asked her to call him.

One month later, Lisa called. Soon afterward, Ashley went on her first **audition.** She got a job in a commercial for the department store JCPenney. Before long, Ashley was working steadily, acting in commercials and posing for print ads.

As a popular star, Ashley is often seen at movie premieres. Still she is a normal girl who likes to curl up at home in her pajamas and watch movies. "I'm not a party person at all," she says.

At Home and Away

Ashley's career got off to a fast start. She was in eight national television commercials before she was eight years old.

Despite her success, Ashley still had a normal life at home. She helped around the house and went to school. She took piano lessons and spent time with friends. When she got older, she worked part-time at clothing stores in the mall. "My dad wanted me to know how long it took to make money and not to take anything for granted. I'm so happy that I've been able to experience a normal life."

One of her favorite activities was cheerleading. When she was eight years old, Ashley joined the Pop Warner cheerleading squad in her hometown. Jennifer was on the squad too. The squad cheered at football games all over New Jersey. Ashley loved performing in front of crowds!

Meanwhile, Ashley auditioned for a touring company of the **Broadway musical** *Les Misérables* (lay mih-zer-AHB). Many people did not think Ashley could do such a big job.

Les Misérables is a popular Broadway show. Ashley toured with the show for a year and a half. It was a big step for a little girl to sing and act in front of an audience every night, but Ashley had the confidence to do it.

She had never had a singing lesson. Could she really sing and act onstage in front of thousands of people?

Ashley could! She did well on the audition and got the job. She was so nervous the first night that, she said, "my legs were quivering." Even so, she loved being onstage.

Ashley toured with *Les Misérables* for a year and a half. Then she spent four weeks in Korea as the star of another musical, *Annie.*

Being in Broadway shows gave Ashley one of her most exciting experiences. She was part of a group called Broadway Kids, which performed at the White House. "We sang Broadway tunes and met the President," Ashley said, referring to President Bill Clinton. "I was so nervous, but it was really fun."

When Ashley came back from Korea, she had a plan. "I wanted to do TV shows," she said. "That's when we started to go back and forth between California and New Jersey."

It didn't take long for Ashley to get a job on TV. Her first TV appearance was on the show *Smart Guy.* Ashley quickly went on to appear as a guest star on *7th Heaven, Grounded for Life, Boston Public, Charmed,* and *Beverly Hills 90210.* Her parents decided that she had a great future in television. The whole family moved to California when Ashley was in eighth grade so that she could go after her dreams.

Even though she was on TV, Ashley went to a public high school. However, she was not popular with the school's drama club. "I didn't get along too well with the drama teachers," she said. "They never wanted to **cast** me in any parts." She missed a lot of school to go to television auditions. She believed the teachers "didn't like me going on the auditions, so I never got selected for the plays."

Ashley did not let **rejection** at school bother her. By the time she was sixteen, she had appeared in several movies and many television shows. Her life was about to take a new turn.

Ashley enjoys helping others. In October 2005, she attended a charity event for New Leash on Life, which benefits homeless animals. This dog was rescued from Hurricane Katrina.

Brenda Song, Dylan and Cole Sprouse, and Ashley were costars on *The Suite Life of Zack and Cody.* The show made Ashley very popular with young people.

Ashley's Suite Life

In 2005, Ashley landed a role on *The Suite Life of Zack and Cody* on the Disney Channel. The show is about twin boys, played by Dylan and Cole Sprouse, who live with their mother in a fancy hotel. Ashley plays Maddie Fitzpatrick, who works at the candy counter in the hotel. She also baby-sits the boys and gets drawn into their crazy adventures.

Ashley had a wonderful time working on *The Suite Life.* "It's a fun show because the kids actually get to star in it," she said. "I'm also excited because the show is taped in front of an audience. I love doing comedy in front of an

On the set of *The Suite Life of Zack and Cody,* Ashley became close friends with costar Brenda Song. "On our lunch breaks we go shopping and get our nails done," Ashley said at the time.

audience and getting the rush of energy that provides."

Ashley also enjoyed the people she worked with. She became especially close to Brenda Song, who plays London Tipton, the spoiled daughter of the hotel's owner. "Brenda and I are like sisters," she explained. "It's the

After costarring in dozens of episodes of *The Suite Life,* Ashley was ready to audition for *High School Musical.*

coolest thing to get to work with my best friend."

The Suite Life of Zack and Cody became a big hit. People began to notice Ashley. Some of the people who saw her were casting a new movie for the Disney Channel. The name of that movie was *High School Musical.*

High School Musical stars (front row, left to right) Corbin Bleu, Lucas Grabeel, and Zac Efron; (back row, left to right) Vanessa Hudgens, Monique Coleman, and Ashley Tisdale. "The movie has a really good message and it's so much fun!" Ashley said. In her real-life high school, her favorite subject was English. Her least favorite subject was math.

Rock to the Top

High School Musical tells the story of an athletic boy and a shy, brainy girl who become the unlikely stars of a high school play. Because these characters break out of the roles they have always played, they force all the students to look at each other and themselves in a new way.

The movie had a large cast, and directors auditioned many different people to fill the parts. The movie's producer, Bill Borden, had seen Ashley on *The Suite Life.* He knew she was talented. However, he still had to make sure she was right for a part in this movie.

The role in the movie "wasn't given to me," Ashley said. "A lot of people think [I got the part] because I'm on Disney, but I had to go on the audition."

Ashley landed the role of drama queen Sharpay Evans. The role was very different from the part of Maddie on *The Suite Life.* "Maddie's really sweet, and Sharpay is just the total opposite," Ashley explained. "She's a mean girl. But the thing I can relate to is, she has this drive—it doesn't matter if people don't think she's the best dancer or performer because she thinks she is." Ashley enjoyed playing someone who is so different from herself.

High School Musical **premiered** on the Disney Channel on Friday, January 20, 2006. More than seven million people watched. The movie was a huge hit! Viewers enjoyed the story and the catchy music and dance numbers. They also responded to the movie's message that it is important to be true to yourself, no matter what other people think about you.

The movie helped start a singing career for Ashley. Nine songs from the movie's sound track went on to become hits, including "What I've Been Looking For" and "Bop to the Top." These songs were performed by Ashley and her **costar**, Lucas Grabeel. Ashley was thrilled to have two songs on the Billboard Hot 100 chart. "The weirdest thing was looking at the Billboard charts and seeing Beyoncé and Sean Paul and then seeing Ashley Tisdale." She went on to record her own CD, *Headstrong,* which entered the Billboard charts at number 5.

High School Musical was so popular that Disney quickly signed the cast and directors to do a **sequel**. *High School Musical 2* premiered on the Disney Channel in August 2007 and was also a big hit. The cast toured and performed the songs from the movie in concerts all over the United States. In the spring of 2008, *High School Musical 3: Senior Year* was filmed. Unlike the first two movies in the series, this one would be released in theaters.

Ashley has been busy with other projects as well. Although *The Suite Life of Zack and*

In July 2007, Ashley and Vanessa Hudgens attended the premiere of the movie *Hairspray*. Ashley often appears in public with other cast members from *High School Musical*.

Cody ended in 2008, that year Ashley began voicing the part of Candice on the Disney Channel cartoon *Phineas and Ferb*.

Ashley Tisdale has become a hot young star. Although she loves being famous, she also knows what is really important in life. Unlike other young stars, she is not a party girl. "I'm not really comfortable in situations at parties and stuff. The whole club scene is not fun for me," she told *Seventeen* magazine. "All I could think about is being at home in my pajamas and watching a movie."

Ashley also remains close to her family. She is active in helping others and has worked with several **charity** events, including A Time for Heroes Celebrity Carnival and the Starlight Starbright Foundation's Winter Wonderland, both of which benefit seriously ill children. It is exactly these normal, down-to-earth qualities that help make Ashley Tisdale such a bright young star.

CHRONOLOGY

1985   Ashley Michelle Tisdale is born in New Jersey on July 2.

1988   Ashley is discovered at a local mall by talent manager Bill Perlman; she appears in her first national TV commercial for JCPenney.

1993–1995   Ashley plays the role of Cosette in a touring production of *Les Misérables.*

1995   She plays the title role in a touring production of *Annie.*

1997–2005   She guest stars on a number of popular television shows.

2001   She is nominated for a Young Artist Award for Best Performance in a TV Drama Series, Guest Starring Young Actress, for her role in *Boston Public.*

2005   Ashley appears as Maddie Fitzpatrick on the Disney Channel series *The Suite Life of Zack and Cody*—a role she will play for three seasons.

2006   She stars as Sharpay Evans in the Disney Channel movie *High School Musical.*

2007   She plays Sharpay Evans in *High School Musical 2;* she tours with the cast in a concert version of the movie; she releases her first CD, *Headstrong;* in November, she has surgery to repair and straighten her nose.

2008   Ashley plays Sharpay Evans in *High School Musical 3;* she voices the part of Candice in the Disney Channel cartoon *Phineas and Ferb.* She begins filming *They Came from Upstairs.*

FILMOGRAPHY

2009 *They Came from Upstairs*

2008 *High School Musical 3: Senior Year*
Picture This!

2007 *High School Musical 2*

2006 *High School Musical*

2002 *The Mayor of Oyster Bay*

2001 *Donnie Darko*
Nathan's Choice

1998 *A Bug's Life* (voice)

1995 *Whisper of the Heart*

DISCOGRAPHY

2007 *Headstrong*

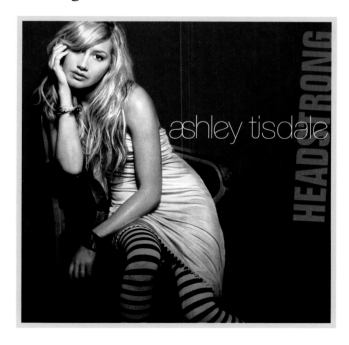

FIND OUT MORE

Books

Disney. *High School Musical All Access.* New York: Disney Press, 2007.

Norwich, Grace. *Ashley Tisdale: Life Is Sweet!* New York: Price Stern Sloan, 2006.

Thomas, Scott. *All in This Together: The Unofficial Story of* High School Musical. Toronto: ECW Press, 2007.

Works Consulted

Brokaw, Francine. " 'Don't Ever Give Up.' " *The Miami Herald,* July 2005.

Eagleson, Kelly. "Ashley Tisdale." *Seventeen,* July 2006.

Geragotelis, Brittany. "Livin' the Suite Life." *American Cheerleader,* February 2006.

"High School Musical's Ashley Tisdale." *People,* April 10, 2006.

Tan, Michelle, and Monica Rizzo. "'I Like How I Look!'" *People,* January 28, 2008.

On the Internet

Disney.com
   www.disney.com
Official Ashley Tisdale Home Page
   www.ashleytisdale.com
Official Ashley Tisdale Music Site
   www.ashleymusic.com
Starlight Starbright Foundation
   www.starlight.org/

GLOSSARY

audition (AW-dih-shun)—To try out for a part in a play, concert, or movie.

Broadway (BRAWD-way)—Live-performance theaters in New York City.

cast (KAST)—A group of people in a play or movie; to assign someone a part in a play or movie.

celebrities (suh-LEB-ruh-teez)—Famous people.

charity (CHAA-ruh-tee)—An organization that raises money to help people in need.

costar (KOH-star)—An actor who performs in a show with another actor.

denying (duh-NY-ing)—Saying something is not true.

musical (MYOO-zuh-kul)—A play or movie that includes singing and dancing.

premiered (pruh-MEERD)—Shown for the first time.

rejection (rih-JEK-shun)—Getting turned away.

sequel (SEE-kwul)—A book or movie that continues the story from an earlier work.

surgery (SUR-jur-ee)—A medical operation in which the skin is cut, then sewn back together.

tour (TOOR)—A trip to different places to perform.

INDEX